On the Railway

written by John Denton
illustrated by Peter Gregory

Puffin Books

Puffin Books, Penguin Books Ltd,
Harmondsworth, Middlesex, England
Penguin Books Inc., 7110 Ambassador Road,
Baltimore, Maryland 21207, U.S.A.
Penguin Books Australia Ltd, Ringwood,
Victoria, Australia
Penguin Books Canada Ltd, 41 Steelcase Road West,
Markham, Ontario, Canada
Penguin Books (N.Z.) Ltd, 182-190 Wairau Road,
Auckland 10, New Zealand

First published by Puffin Books 1976

Text copyright © John Denton, 1976
Illustrations copyright © Peter Gregory, 1976

Printed in Great Britain by
Colour Reproductions Ltd, Billericay, Essex, England

Acknowledgements

British Railways Board, Canadian Pacific
Railways, Festiniog Railway Company, French
National Railways, German Federal Railways,
Japan Information Centre, London Transport,
National Coal Board, Swiss National Tourist
Office, Union Pacific Railroad.

One hundred years ago, travelling across America
could be a dangerous business.
Herds of buffalo might charge across the track.
Indians might attack the '**plenty-wagon-no-horse**'.
Robbers might try to steal the boxes of gold or money
that were often carried by train.

plenty-wagon-no-horse: this is what the Indians
called the train.

French gas-turbine locomotive

Nowadays a train journey is not usually so exciting.
But it can be very much quicker.
This French gas-turbine locomotive
has reached a speed of 318 k.p.h.

Passengers arriving at Waterloo Station, London

Passenger trains carry people,
often at high speeds and between big cities.
They also bring millions of people to work
in the centres of big cities all over the world.

This Union Pacific gas-turbine-hauled freight train
has three engines

Freight trains carry things.
A large lorry can carry about 30 tonnes.
A long freight train can carry several *thousand* tonnes.
It may need several locomotives
to haul such a gigantic load.

points and crossovers at a rail junction

Trains run on **tracks**.
Railwaymen call the track **the road**.
But a train cannot use the track as a car uses the road.
It must always go where the track leads it.

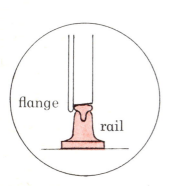

flange

rail

Points and **crossovers** lead
from one track to another.
The flanged wheels of the train
must always follow
where the track leads.

the train is kept on the track
by a flange on the outside of the wheel

7

Locomotives cannot pull trains up steep hills.
The slopes, or **gradients** as they are called,
must always be gentle ones.
As the track cannot go up hills
it has to go through them.

It does this by **cuttings** and **tunnels**.
To cross valleys and rivers
the track is carried
by **embankments**, **viaducts** and **bridges**.

Yes, this is just one freight train!
It is zig-zagging through
a **spiral tunnel**
in the Canadian Rockies.

Every day railwaymen make certain
that the track is safe. They replace worn out rails.
They repack the **ballast** under the **sleepers**.
Heavy trains roaring down the track
make the ballast move. For all these jobs
there are now machines to help the men.

Signals tell the train driver
if the track ahead is clear.
On the early railways
a railway policeman
would stop the train
with a flag or semaphore signal.

The powerful lights
of a modern signal can be seen
nearly 2 kilometres away.
It takes a 1,000-tonne train
travelling at 160 k.p.h.
almost 1.5 kms to come to a stop.

A Victorian
railway signalman

Modern signal

In a modern signalbox
signalmen control many kilometres of track.
The lights on the panel in front of them
show where the trains are.

The first trains
were drawn
by horses.

One of
the earliest
steam locomotives
was the
famous **Rocket**
built by
George Stephenson
and his son Robert.

1. Early horse-drawn railway
2. Stephenson's Rocket
3. Early American
   wood-burning locomotive
4. Early British 'single-driver

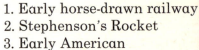

For over 100 years
most locomotives
were powered by steam

The world record
for a steam locomotive
is the 126 m.p.h.
set by the Mallard
in 1938.

In some countries
steam locomotives
still haul
most of the trains.

5. British Railways
   'West Country' Pacific
6. A4 Pacific LNER 'Mallard'
7. French class S 4-6-4
   streamlined steam locomotive
8. American streamlined
   steam locomotive

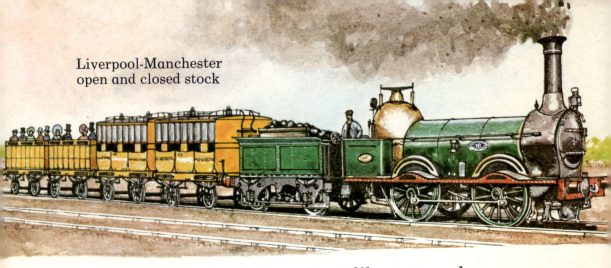

Liverpool-Manchester
open and closed stock

Imagine what it must have been like to travel
in an open coach on one of the early trains,
with the sparks and smoke flying from the locomotive!
Or when it was raining!

Coaches soon became
more comfortable.
For the long journeys
across North America
the American,
George Pullman, built
the first dining
and sleeping cars.

Early Pullman car

Modern dining-car
and sleeping compartment

Nowadays
on some trains
you can have meals,
and sleep.

This **observation car**
on a German express train
gives a very clear view
of the passing countryside.

Observation car on a German train

Most locomotives today are powered
by **electric, diesel** or **gas turbine** engines.

rear
cab

brake resistors

brake
resistors

main
trans-
former

battery charger

Cutaway of modern
British Railways electric locomotive

Electricity is brought to the locomotive by overhead wires
or by a third rail running beside the usual two.

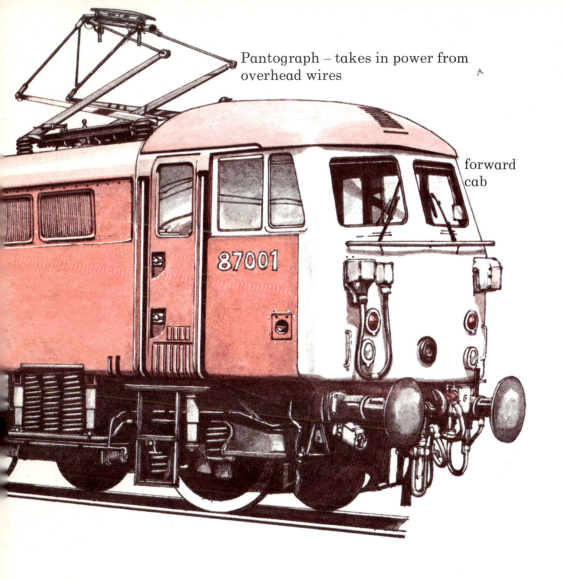

Pantograph – takes in power from overhead wires

forward cab

87001

Electrifying a line is expensive
so diesels, which run on oil, are used on many railways.

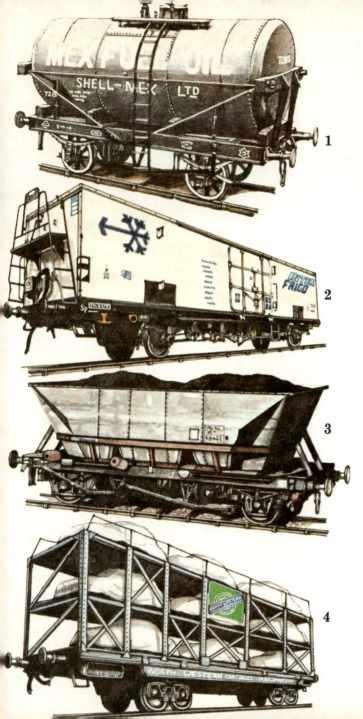

There are many special wagons built for carrying freight. **Tankers** carry oil and other liquids.

Refrigerated vans carry food.

Special **coal wagons** empty their load through a bottom door.

Transporter wagons carry cars . . .

1. Oil tanker
2. Refrigerated van
3. Coal wagon
4. Car transporter

A lot of freight
is sent in **containers**.
These are taken by truck
to a freight terminal
and then lifted
on to a railway wagon
by crane.

The Americans
have **piggy-back trailers**
which are lifted bodily
on to special wagons.

There are special
mail trains
in which postmen
sort the mail
while the train
is going along.

On all trains there is
a van for the guard.

5. Container wagon
6. American piggy-back trailer
7. Mail van on a passenger train
8. Guard's brake van

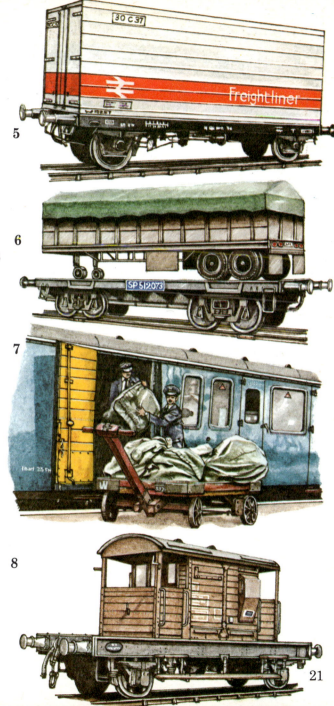

A 'Merry-go-round' train being loaded with coal

Enormous quantities of coal are carried by trains.
Much of it goes direct from the mines to power stations,
where it is turned into electricity. The coal is carried
in '**Merry-go-round**' trains, which are loaded
by overhead chutes at the coalmine and emptied,
through the bottom door of the wagon, at the power stations.

Many wagons have more complicated journeys. The wagons are carefully put in the right order for unloading at a **marshalling yard**. You cannot suddenly take out a wagon from the middle of a long train when it reaches the end of its journey.

Marshalling yard at night

Big cities need big **stations**. With hundreds
of thousands of people using them each day
they must be designed so that people
can get on and off the trains as easily as possible.

Here are some electric locomotives waiting to take trains
out of London's Euston station.

Freight goes through freight terminals.
This **container terminal** is in America.

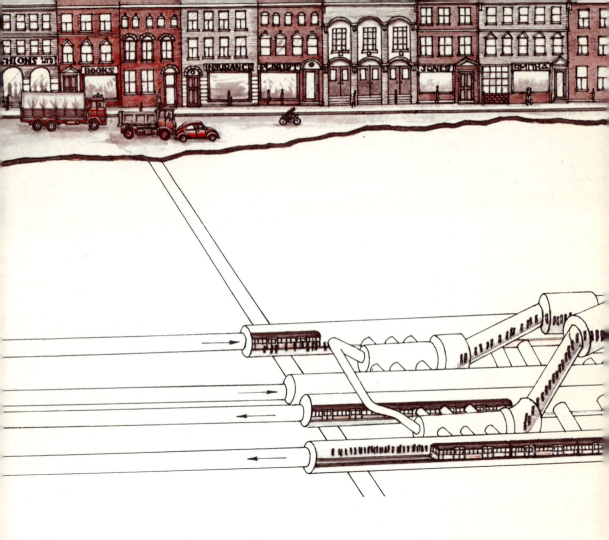

The quickest way to get across
the centre of a big city
is underground – beneath the traffic jams.
It is very expensive to build **underground railways**,
but many big cities now have one.

A busy station may have to have
tunnels to take passengers to six different lines.
Many underground railways now run automatically.
The train stops automatically
at a red signal or at a station.

We have seen that trains usually go up gentle gradients.
Some *have* to go up steep ones.
Some mountain railways are powered
by ordinary electric locomotives. On steeper slopes
they are drawn up the mountain by a wire cable.

And in the Welsh hills the little steam engines
of the Festiniog Railway still puff up the steep gradients,
under their own power.

One of the fastest train journeys in the world
is between Tokyo and Osaka in Japan.
On the specially built track
the trains cover the 560 kms between the two cities
in just over three hours – 3 kms every minute.
Here is an express train with Mount Fuji in the background.

British Rail's Advanced Passenger Train

British Rail's Advanced Passenger Train tilts
so that it can go round corners at high speeds.
It has a top speed of over 250 k.p.h.
These locomotives could draw trains at up to 400 k.p.h.
But at this terrific speed the trains
would have to run on special tracks.

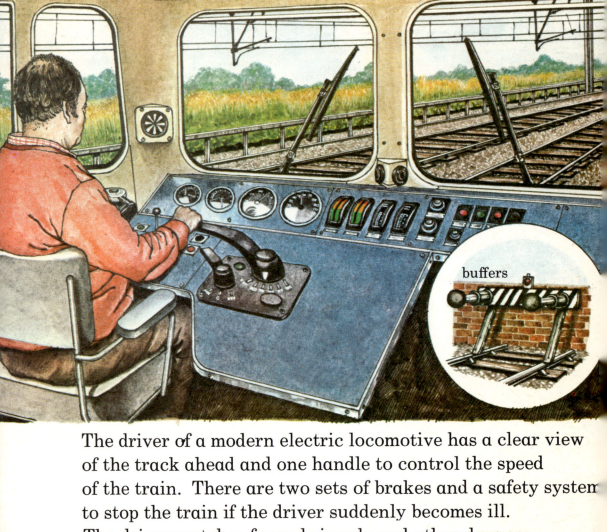

buffers

The driver of a modern electric locomotive has a clear view
of the track ahead and one handle to control the speed
of the train. There are two sets of brakes and a safety system
to stop the train if the driver suddenly becomes ill.
The driver watches for red signals and other dangers
and must bring the train safely, and on time, to the end
of its journey. There are buffers to stop the train
running off the end of the line.